KEVIN M

FIVE
MINUTE
MINDSHIFTS

SHORT, ACTIONABLE ADVICE TO LIVE A POSITIVE, FULFILLED LIFE

FIVE MINUTE MINDSHIFTS

Five Minute Mindshifts © Copyright 2021 Hayfield Press.

Kevin M Cavanagh asserts the moral right to be identified as the author of this work. All rights reserved. No part of this publication may be reproduced, stored in a retrieval system, or transmitted, in any form or by any means, photocopying, recording, electronic or mechanical methods, or otherwise without the prior written permission of the publisher, except in the case of brief quotations embodied in critical reviews and certain other non-commercial uses permitted by copyright law.

Although the author and publisher have made every effort to ensure that the information in this book was correct at press time, the author and publisher do not assume and hereby disclaim any liability to any party for any loss, damage, or disruption caused by errors or omissions, whether such errors or omissions result from negligence, accident, or any other cause.

Neither the author nor the publisher assumes any responsibility or liability whatsoever on behalf of the consumer or reader of this material. Any perceived slight of any individual or organisation is purely unintentional.
The resources in this book are provided for informational purposes only and should not be used to replace the specialised training and professional judgment of a health care or mental health care professional.

Neither the author nor the publisher can be held responsible for the use of the information provided within this book.

A catalogue record for this book is available from the British Library.

FIRST EDITION
ISBN: 978-1-8384162-0-1

Dedication

I dedicate this book to my parents. To my mum, Margaret Cavanagh, for being the kindest and most positive person I know. I was fortunate to be brought up in an environment that taught me to see the positive side of anything and any situation, a skill for which I am deeply thankful. To my late father, Michael Cavanagh, for being the sounding board I often needed as I seek my way in life. Your words of wisdom still ring out in my head today, and your guidance will always be with me.

Acknowledgements

There are a bunch of people who have helped me in my journey to get this book published. I am thankful to every one of you. Without you all, I wouldn't have gotten here.

I managed to cajole a group of people into an unofficial focus group. When formulating the idea of writing a book, I started to throw some early ideas out to them to get feedback. Jane and Nigel Ramsey, Steve McNulty, Ralph Evans, Ben Cooper, Kishore Meda, Paul Wright, Justin O'Dwyer, Alex and Ellen Dailey, and Ed Durham. Thank you all for getting involved and responding to my ramblings and emails. The feedback you gave me was invaluable and though I ignored all of it (that's not actually true!), I was thankful that you were there for me.

To my coach, Hazel Brown. How on earth you understand what I'm thinking and process it into actionable advice, I will never know. What a fun journey, I've learnt a lot and am still learning. Thank you.

My gorilla marketing team. The power of a network is evident. I thank you all for your advice on book titles and subtitles. Ula Koper, Sarah Hinchliffe, Bob Dearsley, Matt Bythell, and Melanie Cains.

To my photographer, Sophie Cooper. What fun we had doing an impromptu photo-shoot. As you can see, the results were fantastic, and there was literally no airbrushing involved!

My publishing team, Kemone Brown and Alyssa Masilungan. Awesome work helping me craft and finesse my ramblings into something representative of a real book.

And finally, to my wife, Charlotte, and my two amazing sons. Thank you for putting up with incessant chatter about this book. You have supported me unreservedly from a dream through to getting this book published. I am truly blessed to have you in my life. Now, are you ready for the next book!

Foreword

For more than 20 years, I have worked with thousands of people worldwide, inspiring, motivating and encouraging them to take positive strides in their work and personal lives. I am fortunate to have worked with various people from school children to the CEOs of FTSE 100 and Fortune 500 companies. One thing has always been clear to me, and that is that we all have enormous potential. With a little knowledge and some helpful techniques, we all have the opportunity to break through boundaries and become the best we can.

I first came across Kevin in the height of the coronavirus pandemic in the summer of 2020. His passion to do something different to inspire and motivate people was apparent. His enthusiasm for self-improvement in all areas of work and personal life is infectious. He has a talent and a friendly, compelling style that makes his material easy to grasp. I love how this book is designed to be read in just a few minutes each day to fit in with the readers' busy lives.

Though the subject of self-improvement has been much covered over the years, this book gives a refreshing new twist on the matter. Kevin has crafted actionable advice that can ignite people to make immediate changes in their lives along with his favourite motivational quotes. It has a simple 'this is what you can do right now' approach to help people achieve goals and make meaningful changes in their work and personal lives. This makes for an inspiring, easy to read book. It provides the tools and techniques to transform your mindset and enrich the quality of life for each of us.

Today, I see the need for us all to be inspired in our lives more than ever. Modern lifestyles can consume much of our energy and mental capacity. Layer on top of this new challenges such as the Coronavirus pandemic of 2020, and we see many businesses and people have had to change quickly and adapt to new ways of working and living. As the Greek philosopher Heraclitus once said, "Change is the only constant in life." Whenever there is change, there is also an opportunity for people; the opportunity to change your mindset, your work and your goals in life.

Through my work, I have seen the transformational difference, which can be achieved. A book like this can shift your mindset and give you the tools to reach your full potential in work and life. A Five Minute Mindshift would benefit us all!

Nigel Risner – international best-selling author: The Impact Code, It's a Zoo Around Here, Zoo Keeper Rules for the Office and You Had Me at Hello.

Introduction

We all have busy lives, right? The modern world moves at a furious pace, and everyone is so busy. It is all too easy to get swept along and, before you know it, days, months, even years have already flown by. I bet you don't even have time to read a book? But with a copy of this book in your hand, let me tell you that this book is different. Forget about the long technicalities and stories. I know that we are too preoccupied for that. Instead, this book is packed with short, daily advice to give you the inspiration and tools you need to go after your life goals with purpose.

The human brain has not changed much for thousands of years. What has changed are the thoughts with which we fill it. Weighing in at 1.4kg and consuming about 20% of our body's energy, our brain is the most powerful organ in our body.[1] It helps ordinary people achieve extraordinary things in their lives by simply learning and acknowledging the power of their minds. This book shares what I've learnt about how small shifts in our mindset can help us achieve a purposeful and successful life.

For over 25 years, I have been fascinated by the power of the mind. This book is the culmination of years of developing myself, setting and achieving life goals, and making myself a more positive, fulfilled person. Nowadays, we often see unhappy and unfulfilled people struggling with job dissatisfaction that even affects their personal lives. I often see people losing motivation, people wanting more but settling for less. Understanding how it feels to be in their position, I wanted to share the simple tools and techniques that have worked for me and, consequently, could also give you the results that you desire. Be that in your career, relationships, finances, or health, the principles remain the same. The rewards are life-changing, not only for you but potentially for those around you too.

Each page has an inspirational quote with a narrative of how you can immediately put the lessons into practice. If you follow these inspirations and take actions as I did, you will experience a big step forward in your life. I know your schedule is tight, so this book has been deliberately designed to keep each narrative short and easy to digest. We learn in different ways, so some themes are intentionally mentioned several times to give the readers alternative approaches to taking them on board.

The book is conceptualized and designed so you can read one page each day for 90 days—which is definitely achievable no matter how busy you are. It will only take a couple of minutes, and it will spark your mind into action. Of course, should you want to go ahead and binge read multiple pages in a day, that would be fine as well.

To get the most of this book, you may wish to place it somewhere you will easily see it to develop the habit of reading it each day. Use it as a source of inspiration and action. Associate it with an already established routine such as while having your breakfast, immediately after waking up, whenever you are in the toilet, or after brushing your teeth. There is no limitation; just be sure to be consistent. You can also set a reminder on your phone if you are a forgetful person! No matter how you prefer to do it, what's important is you get into the habit of reading the book each day.

Following this book will give you the potential to change your life forever, and that is a promise! You may be looking for a small change in life or pursuing a big one; it all depends on you. But one thing is for sure; it will change your life in a meaningful way. The key is to take on board the actions and start shifting your mind to a better place. So, ask yourself this question: Are you prepared to invest a few minutes each day to read this book, to change your life forever?

1

"Life isn't about finding yourself. Life is about creating yourself."

- GEORGE BERNARD SHAW

Many of us go through life looking for something. Something better, more meaningful, more rewarding. But what is the thing that we search for? How would we know if we have already found it?

The truth is, searching for better things in life is never-ending. After achieving one, you would realise that there is another thing to chase. The more you pursue it, the more exhausted you'd be. So, what shall you do then? Well, you must understand that the best way to reach that meaningful, more rewarding life is to create it yourself!

No one is going to do it for you. If you are just getting through life, bumbling along, waiting for some miracle to happen, know that it's not going to happen! You need to get off your behind and go and create the life you want.

Did you know that every person gets to live on this planet for an average of 3754 weeks?[2] Now, I don't know how many of those 3754 weeks you have used up, and that is not important here. What is essential if you want to change is that you focus on it, and start the change NOW. Stop going through the motions of life. Don't wait any longer. Invest the time in yourself and create the life you want. By doing so, a life full of purpose and fulfilment awaits you.

Twenty-five years ago, I discovered I could choose how I perceived my life, and as such, I had the power to change and align it to whatever I want to achieve in life. I started working on myself, making myself a more positive person with a clear purpose and life goals. This book shares many of the quotes and techniques that have worked for me along the way.

These quotes and techniques can also help you in creating the life that you want to have.

2

"You don't have to be great to start, but you have to start to be great."

- ZIG ZIGLAR

Like many things in life, I bet you don't have it all figured out yet? The truth is, most of us don't. In fact, many prominent and successful people known to have achieved great things also started as ordinary people. However, what differentiates them from the majority of the population is that they had giant dreams, passions, and desires. On top of that, they took action; they courageously faced the uncertainties of starting.

Often, before making a decision, the human mind spends far too much time and energy analysing whether our choices would yield good or bad outcomes, and that is understandable. You can spend time and energy thinking about it. But once you have made a decision, you free up all that brainpower to focus on achieving your goals. Your dream may be big and overwhelming, so it would be easier to break it down into smaller tasks and start working from there. If you want to be a professional tennis player, you don't start at the All-England Lawn Tennis Club; instead, you start lower down and work your way up in little steps.

So, for today, take the necessary time and space to think about what you want in life. Don't restrict yourself. There is no limit, so you might as well think big! Look at yourself in the mirror and commit that you want to make a change. There is no doubt that the first step of any journey is the hardest. But what is essential is that you face the fear and uncertainties and commit to yourself in your mind that by beginning your journey, you are on your way to becoming great!

Vision
What do you want for your life?

Think big. Imagine your future in 5 or 10 years. What would your life look like? Where would you be? Who would be there with you? Write your vision here. Keep coming back to it and refine it until you are clear.

3

"It's not enough to have lived. We should be determined to live for something."

- WINSTON S CHURCHILL

One of the greatest gifts as a human is the ability to choose how to live your life. We all have a purpose. Sometimes, we just need to work hard to find out what it is. What is the 'why' behind everything you do? Once you find out, you would feel very empowered, and your path forward will become so much clearer.

So, take the time to discover your purpose. Write down ideas of what you think your purpose is. Most likely, it is buried within you, just waiting to be recognised. You are a capable person. There are lives ready to be impacted by who you are. Your purpose might be to entertain, to teach, to create, or even to break a record.

Regardless of when you discover your purpose, you will suddenly notice capabilities sitting around, just waiting to be discovered. You've heard it before. You only live once, so make sure you make it meaningful.

What is your purpose in life?

What is the thing that lights you up, that you love doing? What are you great at? What do you want people to remember about you? Write your purpose here. Keep coming back to it and refine it until you are clear.

4

"If you don't actively work on your destination, you won't get there."

— KEVIN M CAVANAGH

Imagine you set sail on a boat. You have all the kit and provisions you need—food, water, blankets, and medical supplies. You have everything ready aside from one thing; you have no destination mapped out. I guarantee that you will not get to where you want to be if you don't set yourself an exact destination. Sadly, this is what many of us do in our lives.

Have you ever dreamed of achieving something that seems too impossible? The first challenge is to work out where you want to get to and set yourself goals. Set big scary ones to challenge yourself. Set smaller ones to keep you motivated. Ask these questions to yourself. What do you really want? Where do you want to be in 3, 5, and 10 years? What will make you happy?

Write some goals down on the next page. Aim to have ten initial goals, and once you have them written down, challenge yourself as to why each goal is important to you? Ask this question for each of your goals. Write why each goal is important and discard the ones that you can't come up with an answer. Being unable to answer the 'why' only means that they are not significant in your life right now.

To make your goals more specific, try putting due dates when you plan to achieve the goal. Read these goals every day for each of the 90 days until they are ingrained in your head. By doing this, something magical will happen. Following the Law of Attraction, you will naturally start to make things happen because your goals will gravitate towards you.

What are your goals?

Write down ten goals that you want to achieve. Goals that will help you move towards your purpose and your life vision. Think of large and small goals. If you can't find ten now, schedule some time and come back and add more.

5

"There are two primary choices in life: to accept conditions as they exist, or accept the responsibility for changing them."

- DENIS WAITLEY

Be honest with yourself; how much do you want to change? Are you driven enough to see that change through? You need to have an honest conversation with yourself and make a promise that you will see this through good and bad. Otherwise, you are just wasting your time reading yet another motivational book!

No matter what your situation is, you either accept it, or you change it. You always have a choice in life. Today, take a look at the goals you have written down and spend 5 minutes adding actionable steps in how you can achieve each goal. The actions can be small. Some goals can be more complicated, requiring several actions and steps. Again, the important part is that you are taking responsibility for taking action instead of accepting your life for what it is.

6

"Reality is created by the mind, we can change our reality by changing our mind."

- PLATO, GREEK PHILOSOPHER

Read and re-read this brilliant quote. Think back to when you were a child. Did you ever imagine amazing, out of this world things whilst playing a game? Were you ever a superhero, a god, a superstar? We are all born with an imaginative and open mind. The problem is, as we get older, we stifle this creative mindset and form beliefs about our position in the world.

You have to relearn that you can change your mind. What things do you crave and desire? When reading your goals, visualize what success looks like for each of them. What will it look like? What will it feel, taste, sound like? You change your reality by changing the way you think. Essentially you change your reality by changing your mind.

7

"Be relentless in pursuing your happiness."

- THEO ROSSI

So, you've worked out what you aspire to by setting out your goals. That is a significant step, and commend yourself for a job well done! However, goals are only a set of words on paper unless you become relentless in your drive to achieve them. The difference between dreams and reality is ACTION.

This is where the 'why' becomes essential. Look again at the 'why' that you wrote down beside the goals that you have. Use these 'why's' to motivate yourself, to remind yourself why this journey is important to you. This will make you persistent as you charge after those goals with belief and passion.

You will get there if you keep going. Remember, your 3754 weeks are ticking, and don't waste another one! Be relentless! Keep working towards your goals because even a small step each day matters. When you become relentless, there is no way you will not achieve your goals!

8

"Life is like riding a bicycle, to keep your balance, you must keep moving forwards."

- ALBERT EINSTEIN

Of you are reading one page of this book daily, then by now, you have reached the end of week one. Well done! Give yourself a pat on the back for you have made the foundational steps to shift your mind and your life.

Before we continue, let's have a quick recap. Have you committed to yourself that you want to create something better? Have you set yourself some goals—big and small? Have you written them down and detailed why each goal is important to you? If you can't find a reason why a goal is important to you, did you kick it off the list for now? If you still haven't yet, then do it now.

Are you taking a couple of minutes to read your goals every day? I have a copy of my goals beside my toothbrush to remind me each morning and evening. I read them whilst brushing my teeth; thus, saving me my precious time.

Have you recognized and accepted that you are responsible for creating your life? Are you up for making yourself relentless to achieve these goals?

It would be great to hear about your daily routine for reading your goals. You can get in touch with me at www.kevinmcavanagh.com or on social media.

9

"Be careful how you are talking to yourself, YOU are listening."

- LISA M HAYES

The most important relationship you have in life is the relationship you have with yourself. Let's face it; we live with ourselves every minute of every day. We also spend more time talking internally to ourselves than we do with anyone else. You know, that internal monologue that pops up and says you can't do something, that is also you. We have to learn to live with and love our inner voices. Note that I am not saying you should agree with your inner voice all the time. Constant negative talk from it will have a negative effect on your success.

According to Famira Racy of the Inner Speech Lab at Mount Royal University, your inner voice is like a flashlight into your mind.[3] It can help with emotion regulation, problem-solving, critical thinking, and communicating more effectively. Recognize when it is talking to you in a negative way. One trick is to name it and start talking back positively. Challenge that pessimistic point of view.

Find evidence in your life where you have succeeded and remind your inner voice saying, 'OK, Charlie Chatterbox, I hear you. Think of where you have succeeded in the past and say 'I have decided I will do it anyway and be stronger for it.' This approach helped me with thinking more positively. When I hear my 'Charlie Chatterbox' talking, I find some situation where I succeeded, reframing the whole situation. Remember, talk kindly to yourself; you are important.

10

"Take care of your body, it's the only place you have to live."

- JIM ROHN

We only get one go at this life, and also, we only get one body in which we live this life. Part of the process of valuing yourself is to treasure and take care of yourself. You need your body, as much as your mind, to be in the right place.

Doing some form of exercise is vital for your body and your well-being. It is proven that when we exercise, our bodies release endorphins that lift our mood and happiness levels. It doesn't have to be heavy weight lifting or running a marathon. Start by taking a walk today (you can even listen to a podcast whilst doing it). Take the stairs at work instead of a lift. Get your body moving, even if it's just 10 minutes!

Commit today to find what exercise works for you. Commit to yourself that you will exercise at least three times per week for the rest of these 90 days. Schedule it in your calendar right away! If you do this, you will experience improved physical and emotional health. Start small and build up; the important part is to commit to it and START!

What exercise will I do each week?

Write down your exercise plan. Be specific - how many times will you exercise? What days will you exercise? For how long?

11

"Don't judge each day by the harvest you reap, but by the seeds that you plant."

- ROBERT LOUIS STEVENSON

Sometimes, your goals may seem a long way off, and that is OK. Completing all 90 quotes in this book may seem a long way off, almost daunting. To achieve big dreams, we need to break them down into small, achievable goals. No one succeeds on the first day of their journey.

Think of it this way. Each day you read this book, you are planting a seed and moving on a step ahead. It is similar to how the food on our plate today doesn't appear out of nowhere. It goes through the process of planting, rearing, nurturing long before it can be harvested. After harvest, it would go another long way before we eventually reap the rewards of it.

The same path applies to your life ambitions. Each day you read this book, you will be planting a seed and inspiring your mind to move you forward.

12

"A brand for a company is like a reputation for a person. You earn reputation by trying to do hard things well."

- JEFF BEZOS

There are almost 8 billion people in the world. Every person has unique skills and talents. We are not mass-produced robots, and as such, we have to build our own identities. Building our reputation or personal brand is hugely important in the digital world. The CV will be gone in a few years, and people will look at your personal brand when considering you for a job. Now, this might sound a little strange for a motivational book; however, stick with me as there is a logic here.

Think about your personal brand today. From a personal or work perspective, what do people say about you? What do you want people to say about you? Are you dependable? An expert? Dedicated? Write down some of the key things you want people to remember about you from both a personal and work perspective.

Pick a channel (LinkedIn, Snapchat, Instagram, etc.) and look at what you post there. How are you positioning yourself in this busy, competitive world? It doesn't matter whether you're aspiring to climb the corporate ladder, grow your own small business, or become a zoologist. Whatever you aspire to, a strong personal brand would demonstrate your expertise. How do you want to be perceived? Think of this every time you post anything online. It will help you get to wherever you want to go faster. Remember, there is only one unique version of you.

What do I want my personal brand to be?

How do you want people to remember you? What are the unique features that you want to show the world? Write it down here as though someone was describing you.

13

> "Action is the foundational key to all success."
>
> - PABLO PICASSO

Having good ideas is all well and good. But without actions, ideas are just dreams. Keep a log of ALL your ideas, the small ones, the maybe ones, the downright crazy ones. Whether it is to start the next version of Facebook or completely redesign your garden, writing your ideas down is the first step to identifying the most important ones and making them real.

The crucial thing is to turn your ideas into goals and to attach actions to each of them. As we discussed earlier, breaking down your goal and taking action gives you a path to achieving your goals. Once you have written them down in this book, read them out loud to yourself. Bring them to life and reaffirm whether this is a goal that you want to develop and achieve for your future.

For several years, writing a book was a dream of mine. In late 2019, I started writing a book, but this floundered due to other work commitments. I realised I hadn't set out my goals and action plan for the book; I was just writing my ideas. When I revisited the book in the late summer of 2020, I set out clear goals and, perhaps more importantly, a clear action plan of what I needed to do by when. This focused my mind and helped me get this book completed in just a few months.

14

"Stop plodding,
start performing."

— KEVIN M CAVANAGH

Life is your stage. There is a whole world out there waiting to see what you can do. People need your help, your skills, your experience. Too many of us pass through life without achieving our dreams, and often, many people don't even know what their dreams really are.

The best way to deal with the stage fright of making new things happen is to face it. So, get out there and start performing! Imagine what you would look like and act as if you had already achieved your dreams? Start being that person! Take a look at your goals and your plan. What are you doing today, this week, this month? What actions and necessary steps are you going to take to achieve what you want in your life? It doesn't have to be big, and it doesn't have to be perfect, just start and try…. TODAY!

15

"I am not a product of my circumstances. I am a product of my decisions."

- STEPHEN COVEY

At the beginning of this book, did you commit to reading a page of this book each day? To grow and to learn? Are you sticking to your decision? It is easy to give up and quit, but you owe it to yourself to keep working on yourself each day. It is easy to give ourselves the excuse that our situation is not just ideal, but the reality is that we are greater than our circumstances. If we have the will, there surely will be a way.

It is entirely your decision, but if you half do things, I promise you that you must not expect the entirety of your goal as well. Make that decision to commit to yourself fully, to make things happen in your life. Keep going, and your rewards will surely come.

16

"There's no fear when you're having fun."

— WILL THOMAS

Find your time for fun. When we were still children, we were all uniquely gifted with the ability to have fun. Somehow, we lose this ability as we grow up. So now, find your fun again! We can find enjoyment in the simplest things in life; it is not about having the most money or the fanciest car.

Go search! If you can find fun at work, at home, with your partner, your children, or whatever it is, life becomes much lighter and easier. When it is fun, life is not a chore. Every week, make time for activities that you enjoy and make you happy.

Similarly, spend a couple of minutes to reach out and make someone smile today. Happiness is contagious; when you make someone else smile, it makes you smile too. Life doesn't always have to be serious. Bring out the young child in you and find the fun things in your life.

17

> "A man is but the product of his thoughts. What he thinks, he becomes."
>
> - MAHATMA GANDHI

That are you thinking right now? Has today started with positive or negative thoughts? Remember that the primary cause of unhappiness is never the situation, but the thoughts about it. The whole focus of this book is to get you thinking positively. There are techniques to stop negative thoughts before they take hold of you. One of the most straightforward techniques that works for me is to catch negative thoughts as you think them.

For today, whenever you have a negative thought, immediately write it down on the pages of this book. It could be random thoughts of you being too thin, too fat, not smart enough, not brave enough, not successful enough, or any unhelpful idea. Once you have written it down, question the assumptions, and challenge yourself. Where did it come from? Ask yourself if it's really true? Can you imagine a positive alternative? Write that next to the negative thought.

Practice this regularly and it will become a habit. Eventually, you will retrain your brain to think positively. Smile or laugh—did you know that you can't think negative thoughts whilst smiling?!

What negative thoughts and beliefs do you hold?

Write down your doubts, your negative beliefs, the things that you think you 'can't' do.

18

"Rule your mind
or it will rule you."

- BUDDHA

Have you ever felt like your mind has too many thoughts spinning around it? Too many thoughts that you are not sure what to do first? Our mind is an amazing part of us. In the revised edition of his book 'Quantum Healing', Deepak Chopra supposes that the average person has about 60,000 thoughts per day![4] Just let that sink in for a moment! If you let these thousands of ideas run simultaneously, how can you even function effectively?

A valuable part of investing in yourself is to clear your mind. One great way to do this is through meditation. I know it may sound a bit woo-woo, but trust me, it works! Imagine if you could clear that fog and get complete clarity on what you should be focusing on. Meditation is a great tool to achieve this!

Find a time to meditate and make it a part of your daily routine. Most people meditate in the morning, but the important thing is to find a time that suits you. If time is short, it doesn't have to take long, and there are some great meditation apps like Calm or MyLife. Learn more about meditation and invest that time in yourself. It will make you more productive.

19

"Do one thing every day that scares you."

- MARY SCHMICH

OK, doing something scary every day may be unrealistic, but the principle is that you need to push yourself outside your comfort zone. Just to be clear, it doesn't have to be something that physically scares you! I'm not talking about jumping out of a plane with a parachute (I have tried that once and can confirm it does scare you!).

We all have a comfort zone—a place where we get through every day, keeping our lives within the same routine and normality. To achieve personal growth, it is necessary to smash out of your comfort zone. You need to push yourself a little bit more. Put yourself forward— make an outstanding presentation at work, sign up for that new hobby, apply for that new job. What's the worst that can happen? If you succeed, that's perfect. If you fail, you would still learn.

As your confidence grows, push yourself further. Challenge yourself more. Something that was once scary will seem less daunting. I promise you, you will grow as a person, and you might even enjoy it! So, what are you going to do today to push yourself out of your comfort zone?

20

"Repetitio, repetitio, repetitio."

— ANONYMOUS

My late father used to say, "Repetitio est mater studiorum," Latin for, 'Repetition is the mother of learning,' (and yes, he did know Latin). The only way you are going to get good at things is with continual practice.

No one is born an outstanding person, whether that's in business, sport, or whatever. If you have ambitions of being successful, you need to practice. If you want to be the next LeBron James, Megan Rapinoe, or Adam Peaty, you need to practice. And here is the thing, practice doesn't mean once a month. It means regular; it may be every week, every day, or even several hours each day.

Is there something in your goals that you want to master? Commit to yourself about where you want to get to. Make a plan today! To get there, you will need to schedule and practice it as part of your routine. Remember, it won't happen unless you do this.

21

"I've missed more than 9000 shots in my career. I've lost almost 300 games. Twenty-six times I've been trusted to take the game winning shot and missed. I've failed over and over and over again in my life. And that is why I succeed."

- MICHAEL JORDAN

It may go against your existing beliefs, but failing is a good thing! Failure only shows that you are practicing. Failing is learning. You only really fail when you give up! We all fail at something so be kind to yourself. When you do fail, reposition it in your mind as learning. The important thing is to take time to analyse it and work out what you've learnt.

If you take this approach - and believe failure is learning - you will progress and get stronger, better, and more knowledgeable. Keep believing in yourself even when things go wrong. Pick yourself up and go practice again.

Whilst in my teens, I represented my high school at public speaking. I recall my first speaking competition, one midweek evening at a local school. I arrived at a hall with well over 100 people in it. I still remember the moment it was my turn to speak. I stood up, walked to the podium, stood under the bright lights and froze. Eventually, I mumbled my way through my speech, but it didn't go well. It was a horrible experience; I had failed. However, I learnt from it and have never delivered a presentation again without being thoroughly prepared!

22

"I have been impressed with the urgency of doing. Knowing is not enough; we must apply. Being willing is not enough; we must do."

- LEONARDO DA VINCI

Don't wait for that perfect moment to start because it won't come! If you have your list of goals, are you working towards achieving them? You must take action! If you have nothing but ideas, nothing will change. Every week, make yourself a realistic plan of tasks you can and must achieve. Doing so will move you closer to your goals and what you want in life.

If your goal is enormous and overwhelming, break it down and push yourself to do a small amount each day. Everything you do is a step nearer a goal. The act of doing something and doing it now not only moves you towards your goals, but it also creates momentum—an unstoppable force that will drive you on. Don't put off until tomorrow what can be done today!

23

"Distracted from distraction by distraction."

– T.S. ELIOT

How many hours per day do you spend flicking through Facebook, WhatsApp, Twitter, Instagram, or email? The average American spends just over an hour (64.5 minutes) on Facebook and 48 minutes on Instagram each day.[5] Add that up, and over a week, that is a lot of time distracted and not working for something more productive!

How much time do you spend on social media? Honestly? You may not like to hear this, but if social media is becoming an addiction, you need to cut down on it! It's like a drug. Just to be clear, I am not anti-social media, but I am against it distracting you from your goals.

To guide you through this, many apps can help you monitor your mobile phone activities. Download one and, for a week, track what apps you are using most on your device. The results will give you irrefutable evidence as to whether you need to change your usage.

One quick and simple trick that works for me is to go into your phone settings and turn off notifications for each of these social apps. Do not let the app own you, pinging and notifying you all the time. You decide when to look at them. I find that allocating set times each day for social media is a great way to stop distractions.

24

"Start creating your future today."

- KEVIN M CAVANAGH

Here is the thing, if YOU are not actively creating YOUR future, then your future is creating you! If you have no plan, no direction, no actions for yourself, then the world may just decide it for you.

I did this when I graduated from university. I was fortunate to get three job offers. As a young, inexperienced person, I took the job that paid the most money, with no plan or goal about what I ultimately wanted to achieve in my career. I ended up in a town I hadn't planned to be at, with a role that I hadn't previously considered. Fortunately, things did work out, and I learnt along the way. As I progressed, I made more conscious decisions. But I also realised that it is so easy to be led by life. Incidentally, chasing the money is not a wise long-term plan either, but I will get on to that another time.

Too many of us just coast through life, not achieving our potential. You have to take charge of the direction of your life. Work on motivating yourself to keep pushing and trying to improve yourself continuously. Make it you who decides where you are going. It will give you a purpose, and you will feel great.

25

"Don't get so busy making a living that you forget to make a life."

- DOLLY PARTON

Sorry to break this to you, but as mentioned, the World Health Organisation estimates the average human gets 3754 weeks on this amazing planet.[2] How many have already passed you by?

Do you want to waste your life away? You may have done great things so far, and I'm sure if you think hard, you have achieved so much. Don't just get through life; imagine how good the rest of your life could be with a plan and action?

Keep that belief that you will achieve your goals. Read them each day and take the necessary actions to start achieving them. When you have a purpose, you will be empowered and motivated to make the life you want.

26

"If you're in the room, be in the room."

— NIGEL RISNER

I love this quote from 'The Impact Code' by Nigel Risner. He says that when you are at work, at home with the kids, out with friends, or wherever you are, you must be mentally in that place, at that moment.

Focus on what you are doing at the moment. Do not be distracted by everything else. Stop thinking about all the other stuff you have spinning around in your head and just focus on that moment. If you can master this, it will make you way more productive, and you'll get more out of what you are doing (as will the other people in the room).

I had a lightbulb moment with this quote. Often, whilst putting the children to bed, I would be flicking through BBC news or sports pages on my phone, half listening and half engaging with my children. Then, I realised I was choosing not to be in that moment. The lesson was profound to me—it is so easy to be distracted in the modern world. And the problem is even worsened because we allow ourselves to be distracted; in short, we choose to be distracted. Imagine what you could achieve if you commit not to be distracted?

Practice being physically and mindfully present by intentionally telling yourself to be in the room. Notice when your mind starts wandering and pull yourself back on track to the task you are doing right now. Be in the room.

27

"When you arise in the morning, think of what a precious privilege it is to be alive - to breathe, to think, to enjoy, to love."

- MARCUS AURELIUS

We all run on a 24-hour internal clock known as the circadian day. It helps us go to sleep, wake up, and have peaks of alertness around the same time every day. The times may be different for everyone. Within the circadian day, we go through blocks of productivity and heightened focus. These blocks of productivity time are known as ultradian cycles - when your brain is most switched on and energetic.

For me, I get up at 6 am to make the most of the early morning, having ditched the late night's binge-watching Netflix. That is when I'm most productive. Could this be the same for you? Work out your ultradian cycles. Observe and note down the points in the day when you feel most alert and productive. These are the times to take on the most significant projects or challenges of the day.

You can also make the most of each day by increasing your day. Try setting your alarm 30 minutes earlier, what extra things could you fit in your day? You could take an early morning walk, write a book, read and review your goals or practice journaling. There are many things you could add to your day for that small investment of time. Try it tomorrow, but plan in advance. Decide what you will do with the time. It is a privilege to be in this world. Make sure you are making the most of this privilege.

28

"Be the reason someone smiles today."

– ANONYMOUS

Kindness is often pushed to one side, in favour of other things that seem more important. Simple things can make a real difference to others' lives, and in turn, they also improve your well-being. You may be driven and hungry for success, but don't pursue that at the expense of others around you.

Making someone smile doesn't have to cost you money or take a lot of your time. It could be something as simple as calling a friend you haven't spoken to in a while, hugging someone, or complimenting a friend or a colleague. Kindness costs nothing, but it can reduce stress and improve our mood, self-esteem, and happiness.

Imagine how great the world would be if we all pay a compliment to one person each day. See what you can do to make someone smile today.

29

"You can't start the next chapter of your life if you keep re-reading the last one."

- ANONYMOUS

Sometimes, we get so caught up with our past experiences to the point that they block us from having a successful future. Why do we hold on to the past? Why is it so difficult to let go of past experiences? One of the most basic human needs is survival, and for that, we crave certainty. Our mind builds certainty by using past experiences to predict future outcomes. If we allow ourselves to step into the unknowns of the future, that becomes uncertain. In short, it is this fear of uncertainty we have to push through.

Accept that your past experiences do not always show what future outcomes will be. Recognise the need to move into an unknown future, and this will give you the strength to shift your thinking. When you come across a new challenge, don't let your mind automatically associate it with a past outcome. It doesn't have to be the same if you believe you are changing and are motivated to become better.

Your mind isn't infinite; acknowledge the bad, then move on and fill your mind with the vision of your future.

30

"Surround yourself with individuals that inspire you."

- ROBERT STACK

Now, have you got through 30 quotes? Hopefully, you are getting value out of this book so far and the additional resources on my website.[6] Reading for a few minutes each day is a significant investment in yourself, so keep going!

Have you shared any of these quotes with anyone? Come to think of it, who do you share information with, and who do you surround yourself with? Do you surround yourself with people that inspire you? Do you inspire them in return?

Spend less time with people that drag you down and more time with people who inspire you. Create a network around you. A network that you can spark off. How would that help you progress in your life?

There is great advice coming up, and it will change you! P.S. You are one-third of the way through the book, so now is an ideal time to review your goals. Are they still valid and meaningful to you? Are you still committed to them? If not, question why they are still there? Tweak them, so you have a list of meaningful, actionable goals you are committed to.

31

"Reading is essential for those who seek to rise above the ordinary."

- JIM ROHN

The odds are that you haven't learnt everything in life just from attending school. To grow our minds and our capabilities, we need to feed them with continual learning.

A great way to continually learn is to read non-fiction books. It comes naturally to some, while others have to work on it. Think of books as an experiment. On average, you invest around £10/£15 and some of your time. You might not connect with every book, but books have the power to inspire you and change your life forever.

Make yourself a commitment—challenge yourself to read a book a month. Research and buy several books and then put the time in your daily schedule to read and reflect. I allocate thirty minutes before bed to reading.

Tip: Local libraries can be an excellent source. You can often reserve library books online, so you don't even need to buy them! Or you can get them second hand on websites like eBay.

You can see a list of recommended reading at www.kevinmcavanagh.com/resources.

Books I will read.

Write yourself a list of books you will read in the next six months.

32

"Think for yourself. Trust your own intuition. Another's mind isn't walking your journey, you are."

— ROBERT STACK

Stop listening to all the noise out there on the Internet. Everyone has done everything better, bigger, and are more successful than you are, if you believe it all. You are the master of your destiny. Whilst that may be scary to some, it is inspiring if you think about it. Whilst you are free to listen to others' opinions, you must form your own judgement and make your own decisions.

We were all born good enough to do what we want to do. I repeat you were born good enough! So what if others have done what you want to do? They are not you! They do not have the unique skills and experience that you have. There is only one you.

Ignore all the noise. If it helps, write down a list of things you have achieved in your life. Spot the common theme with them. Did all these achievements happen when you trusted yourself and used your intuition? We can all do it. Ignore all the noise and keep pushing on. You've got this!

Good things I have already achieved.

Write here a list of your achievements – have you ever found a job, passed an exam, stood up to someone, got a home?

33

"Twenty years from now you will be more disappointed by the things that you didn't do than by the ones you did do, so throw off the bowlines, sail away from safe harbor, catch the trade winds in your sails. Explore. Dream. Discover."

- MARK TWAIN

For a moment, imagine yourself 20 years into the future. What age will you be? Where will you be at? What will you be doing? What will you have accomplished?

Every week, month, and year that we wait for that perfect moment to start, we are robbing ourselves of time. I cannot overstate the importance of taking action each day to make progress. Have a go, not everything will work, but you will build unstoppable momentum. Keep pushing yourself. Small steps every day will reap big rewards.

34

"Whatever the mind of man can conceive and believe, it can achieve."

- NAPOLEON HILL

Your mind is a fantastic tool. As discussed previously, when we are children, we believe and imagine many incredible things. Somehow, we go from imagining we can do anything in life to growing up and accepting that often we are just average – average partners, average employees, average achievers.

To break out of this mould, find the time and allocate thirty minutes for quiet contemplation, with no distractions and mobiles switched off. Question your mind about what you truly want to be.

Forget the real-life constraints for a moment. Spend some time with yourself, exploring the what if? Get more in-depth with the thoughts that come into your head and write down the results below. If you find it hard to answer this, try again a few days later and eventually it will come to you. Compare these thoughts to the goals you set initially? Do you see similarities? It will help you conceive who you want to be and what your purpose is in your life.

My dreams of what I can be in life.

What can you imagine for yourself? Write down what you imagine your life could be?

35

"Too many of us are not living our dreams because we are living our fears."

- LES BROWN

We are conditioned to fear things. This is fine whilst we are growing up. It is natural for us to fear the unknown and to protect ourselves from it. It doesn't always serve us well as adults, though.

Here is an interesting reality check; you will not suddenly, magically lose that fear one day. Even the most successful entrepreneurs still have fear when they start something new. The fascinating thing is that they push themselves through that fear.

Often, you feel fear at the thought of doing something, not at the point where you are doing it. If you are held back by fear, write down a list of things you have done that you feared initially. It might be learning to ride a bike, a public presentation, or even climbing a mountain. This is your evidence that you can overcome fears. Whenever you fear something new, look at this list to help push yourself through that fear.

Examples where I have overcome my fear and dome something.

Write down examples of when you have pushed through that fear and gone ahead and done something anyway here.

36

"Nothing is impossible, the word itself says 'I'm possible'!"

- AUDREY HEPBURN

I love this quote, though not in its literal sense as, for sure, some things are impossible to us. I have little chance of being a professional football player as I am already too old! Putting toothpaste back in a tube seems pretty impossible!

The principle here is around changing mindset; if you talk to yourself and say it is impossible, your mind will believe that as fact.

If you change that word slightly to 'I'm possible,' then your whole mindset changes and you would develop the belief that you can achieve something. The next time you face an 'impossible' task, just remind yourself, there is another way. Shift your mindset and see what is possible.

37

"It doesn't matter how many times you fail, you only have to be right once."

- MARK CUBAN

I love this quote. It inspires me every time I read it. Most successful people (I'm not talking just about financial success) have lots of failures along the way. The thing that makes successful people stand out is that they don't dwell on what has not worked, they learn from it and move on.

Successful people like Elon Musk of Tesla Inc. and Jeff Bezos of Amazon didn't get to where they are with just one idea. They are continually failing at things, and each time those failures get them a step closer to success. Why? Because the truth is that you can learn from each failure. You grow with each failure, and as Mark Cuban says, 'You only have to be right once.'

Can you do that? Next time something goes wrong, can you not dwell on it and instead learn from it and move on?

38

"If you look at what you have in life, you'll always have more. If you look at what you don't have in life, you'll never have enough."

- OPRAH WINFREY

Modern living encourages us to compare and look at what others have. It is amplified by social media that makes it easy to compare ourselves with others' 'perfect' lives.

Stop it! It doesn't achieve anything. It doesn't make you feel good and it offers no benefit to you. We all have to learn to be thankful for what we do have; our health, our home, our partner, and our children. Live in your life, not the imaginary world of others who appear to have a perfect life.

39

"Life is 10 percent what happens to me and 90 percent of how
I react to it."

- CHARLES SWINDOLL

Have you ever been in an unideal situation, felt helpless, and thought to yourself, "That is just the way it is," or "Oh, that is just bound to happen." Do yourself a favour and stop accepting these excuses! You have a choice of how you react to everything in life.

When my father passed away, naturally I grieved, but then I choose to fill my mind with happy memories of him and his life. That was a much better place to be in my head. You have a choice as to how you think about every situation.

Try to practice reacting positively to things. Someone cuts you up whilst driving, try not responding, just get back to what you were thinking about on your journey. You will start to see that you can easily alter your thinking which is immensely powerful. Your mind is indeed a powerful asset when you use it in the right way.

40

"The key to success is finding something you like to do, and becoming really good at it."

- MARK CUBAN

I'm considering this quote from a work perspective, though it equally applies to a hobby or something in your personal life.

A recent study by Gallup across 160 countries found that 85% of workers are not engaged in their jobs.[7] This number is staggering! If you are one of that 85%, it is up to you to do something about it because no one else will. I'm not saying quit your job tomorrow and do something radically different. Instead, start to open your eyes to opportunities around you.

What do you like doing? What could you be really good at? Perhaps there is a different role within your company that would interest you or a course you would like to enrol on? Most companies worth their salt would rather have motivated, happy employees in roles in which they excel. Think about it, make a plan, and make that change!

41

"What we fear doing most is usually what we most need to do."

- RALPH WALDO EMERSON

Fear is a massive block to leading the life you deserve. The thing is, if you fear doing something and put it off, it won't suddenly go away. Whether it is a difficult conversation, a decision you are struggling to make, or a change you want to happen. Ask yourself this— what is the worst that can happen if I do the thing I am putting off?

Write it down and then think about what the impact might be? What is the worst that could happen? How would you recover if it did go wrong? And what would the upside be if it did work out? Is that upside not worth more than the fear of what might go wrong?

What things am I putting off due to fear?

Write here the things that are too difficult or too scary for you to take on right now.

42

"I've learned that people will forget what you said, people will forget what you did, but people will never forget how you made them feel."

- MAYA ANGELOU

No matter who we are or what our position in society is, we have an impact on others. Every interaction you have will affect other people, and of course, people matter.

Practice kindness. It is within your gift to make others feel amazing. Treat others as you would like them to treat you. On top of that, there is a further reason to be kind; it has health benefits. Acts of kindness produce oxytocin, which helps lower blood pressure and improve our overall heart health. When dealing with someone today, think about what you can do to be kind to them. Think about how you can make them feel good and happy.

43

"Remember that not getting what you want is sometimes a wonderful stroke of luck."

- DALAI LAMA

In the modern world, we want things instantly. However, sometimes, we have to wait for the best things in life because we won't just get them when we want them. It's not unusual for life to get in the way of our plans.

Remember, it is always your choice how you react. If life throws a curveball at you, it's nothing personal; it's just life! It happens to everyone. Sometimes, what we do get is better for us in the long run. Make a deal with yourself to find the positive in every situation. Life is much better when you react in this way.

44

"Yesterday is gone. Tomorrow has not yet come. We have only today. Let us begin."

- MOTHER TERESA

Such simple yet meaningful words. There is no point dwelling over yesterday, the things you didn't get done, the conversations you had or didn't have. It is today that we need to focus on, this moment, right now.

Where are you heading? Are you committed to where you want to get to? What can you do today to help yourself towards those goals? Even if you are part way through your day, pause, grab a drink and re-read your goals. Planning and action are two of the best stress relievers available to us all.

45

"Focus less on the impression you're making on others and more on the impression you're making on yourself."

- AMY CUDDY

In reality, people are not thinking about you as much as you think they are. However, the importance of how we communicate with ourselves cannot be understated. Many of us know that your body language defines who you are and dictates the impressions you leave on others. What is less known is that body language impacts the impression you are making on yourself as well.

Think of it this way. All along, there is a conversation happening between your body and mind, all the time. Even when you're sleeping, your body is communicating information to your mind. By working on your body language (facial expressions, body posture, gestures, eye contact), you actively impact that conversation's content.

When we practice positive body language, we can carry ourselves in a more powerful way, instructing our feelings, thoughts, and behaviours. It sends messages to our mind, enabling us to feel powerful and present (and even perform better) in situations.

Perhaps we need to stop worrying about the impression we're making on others and instead adjust the impression we've been making on ourselves.

46

"We are what we repeatedly do. Excellence, then, is not an act, but a habit."

- ARISTOTLE

Whether it is physical, mental, or spiritual, we are the sum of our habits. If you keep grabbing that junk food, you will not lose weight. If you do keep doubting yourself, you will not build your confidence. To create a habit, we need to work on ourselves and practice to be the best we can each and every day.

Repeatedly working on shifting your mindset to practice positive thinking will have a significant impact on your life. Practice this by re-reading the negative beliefs you have written down. Are there any more you can add? Concentrate on just one of them at a time and practice replacing it with a positive belief — I will take on that challenge, I am experienced enough, I have the willpower.

47

"Never bend your head. Always hold it high. Look the world straight in the eye."

- HELEN KELLER

A study by Dr Albert Mehrabian in the 1960s concluded that 93% of communication is non-verbal.[8] Have you ever gone into a shop and the shop assistant mumbles without really looking at you? Compare that with the shop where you are greeted by a genuinely confident assistant who smiles, looks you in the eye, and talks to you. Perhaps two very different experiences.

Fifty-five percent of communication is based on body language, so teach yourself to stand up straight. Interestingly, standing straight also improves your voice projection, which accounts for 38% of communication. Before you have an important meeting or interview, take a moment to practice speaking in front of a mirror to see how you communicate, you might be surprised how you come across when you stand up straight!

48

"My favorite things in life don't cost any money. It's really clear that the most precious resource we all have is time."

- STEVE JOBS

We are all blessed with exactly the same amount of time each day. As you get busier and busier, time becomes more precious.

How well do you manage your time? Do you often feel like there is not enough time in the day? Perhaps you continuously work long hours to hit your deadlines? Maybe you even feel too busy that you miss meals and sleep? These are all classic signs that you may not be managing your time effectively.

Benjamin Franklin once said that time is money. Just like money, time must be appropriately managed. For example, it is best to take on more demanding activities in your high-energy times, like when you are at your mental peak. Reserve your low-energy times for small, more straightforward tasks, like responding to emails.

If you plan and manage your time correctly, you will find a balance between work, leisure, and rest. On top of that, you will reduce your stress levels and feel a lot happier.

For an easy time management planner that worked for me, check out www.kevinmcavanagh.com/resources

49

"I learned that courage was not the absence of fear, but the triumph over it. The brave man is not he who does not feel afraid, but he who conquers that fear."

- NELSON MANDELA

So here is a secret, many successful people that you admire also feel fear! Fear doesn't go away as your bank balance grows or you become an expert in your field. Ironically, we often feel fear before we do the thing we are fearful of. When you are actually doing something, the fear usually disappears.

Several years ago, I was fortunate to have experienced a skydive—jumping out of a plane at 10,000 feet, strapped to a bit of material and string. It was arranged the night before, over dinner and a few glasses of wine. When morning came around, fear gripped me and I started thinking "I can't do this, I can't jump out of a plane, what happens if it goes wrong, what happens if I get up there and I can't do it, I don't even like heights!" But once I conquered my fear, I went ahead and found that the experience was terrific. Whilst actually doing it, I had no fear at all.

Fear is always there and we need to recognise it, acknowledge it, and make friends with it. If you do this, the fear won't stop you from pushing ahead. It will simply remind you of the great things you are working to achieve. Pushing yourself in this way is also immensely rewarding, especially as you conquer your fears. Learn to recognise when you feel fear, live with the fear, acknowledge it, and push through it.

50

"There is no easy way from the earth to the stars."

— SENECA

Ever seen an advert on the internet promising instant and effortless success? We've all seen some fantastic offer and been tempted by it, right? The truth is that there is no easy shortcut to anything.

Seneca, the Roman writer, was spot on. You can't become an athlete by sitting on the couch and watching Netflix every day. You can't grow a successful business by being distracted, surfing the Internet each day.

Stop looking for shortcuts and either accept that you will not be the next Sir Richard Branson, or you will have to put in the hard work to get somewhere. Granted there is a difference between hard work and smart work. To transform your life, you need to get your head around the fact that it takes effort and hard work, which has to come from within you.

51

"Above the clouds, the sun is always shining."

- ANONYMOUS

This is one of my favourite quotes of all time. At that moment when everything seems stacked against you, when you are down and out, beaten, tired, and uninspired, remind yourself that above the clouds, the sun is always there. It is still shining like the bright, amazing star it always is. There is always a better day, and there is no doubt that you will get there.

If you can lift the clouds in your mind, you can reach that sunshine of thought, as if you are on an aeroplane flying through the clouds. All it takes is for you to actively lift your thoughts above the clouds and there, you will see sunshine once again.

52

"It is never too late to be what you might have been."

— GEORGE ELLIOTT

No matter what stage of life you are at, do not be discouraged because people grow and succeed at all ages. According to Barclays Bank research in 2017, the fastest-growing age group of business owners between 2006 and 2016 was those aged over 65, with a 140 percent increase.[9]

Many 'silverpreneurs' set up a multi-million-pound business in their 70s. No matter what your dream is, you are never too old and it's never too late. When you define and work on your dream, you will create the rest of your life the way you imagined it to be.

53

"Everything in life is easier when you don't concern yourself with what everybody else is doing."

— ANONYMOUS

We all get caught up in the modern world of comparing ourselves with others—they have a bigger house than us, so and so bought a new car, or the Evans' went to Disney World. It is a natural human instinct to compare ourselves, but comparing yourself is a path to unhappiness. All it does is amplify the things we don't have and we don't like about ourselves and our lives.

Have you experienced this? When was the last time you checked your Facebook or Instagram feed and got envious of someone? A quick mindset shift is to learn to become aware of your triggers and avoid them. If you want to make a success in your life, don't spend time obsessing over how wonderful someone else's life is. Often, it is not as wonderful as they portray it, anyway.

54

"Most people don't want to acknowledge the uncomfortable truth that distraction is always an unhealthy escape from reality."

— NIR EYAL

Distraction is any action we take that is not aligned with what we intended. Do you ever find yourself wasting away days or evenings getting distracted on the Internet? Have you ever spent time going from site to site to site, forgetting what you even started searching for? We often blame technology for distraction, but the root cause often lies within us. If we don't deal with the root causes, we keep finding ways to distract ourselves and continue to be the 'helpless victims.'

I firmly believe that one of the keys to change is altering our habits. I used to be an easily distracted person—my mind wandering off the task at hand and the day passing by. To change, I needed to acknowledge that it wasn't the technology to blame, but my inner drivers and how I managed my time.

55

"Winners are made."

- KEVIN M CAVANAGH

Here is the good news: No one is born with a mindset readily-moulded to succeed in life. Some people do develop more determination than others. Some may have a financial advantage. However, many don't even recognise the advantages they have. You and you alone have this wonderful choice to make your life a success… or not.

We win in many ways, not just in terms of material, financial success. There are many ways we can make ourselves winners and reach happiness and fulfilment in life. If you can learn self-discipline, commitment, and self-kindness, you will learn how to shift your thinking. Subsequently, the amazing life you have always dreamed of will appear. And that is being a winner.

56

"If you hear a voice within you say, 'You cannot paint,' then by all means paint and that voice will be silenced."

- VINCENT VAN GOGH

We all have that voice inside us that tells us, 'You can't do that,' 'That is too hard,' or 'I don't feel like that.' Imagine if you could learn to accept that inner voice but shift your mind so that you can do it anyway.

You can do this, and it is easy for you to achieve. The trick is not to fight it, just accept that the voice is in there. This activates your prefrontal cortex to actively respond and reassure you that you are capable of doing what your mind is telling you that you can't. In other words, it can differentiate these conflicting thoughts rationally. For reference, the prefrontal cortex controls your brain's executive functions such as planning, decision-making, problem-solving, self-control, and acting with long-term goals in mind.

If you've got evidence that you have already done something before, constantly remind yourself of it. If you don't want to go to the gym today, but you felt great after the last time you went, remind yourself of that feeling. Next time your inner voice pops up, acknowledge it, and then crack on with what you were going to do. Push past the inner voice!

57

"Everything you've ever wanted is on the other side of fear."

- GEORGE ADDAIR

Let's be honest. Fear has been around since the times when we were cave dwellers—for a good reason. They had to be constantly alert and fearful of animals that might attack them, rivals that might kill them, and foods that might poison them.

Fortunately for us, our world has progressed since those days and most food in a supermarket won't poison you anymore! Feeling fear is an entirely natural human reaction. Interestingly, when you analyse it, the sensations of fear are exactly the same as the sensations you feel when you are excited.

Conceivably, next time you feel fear, imagine if it might be that you are feeling slight excitement at the prospect of doing something. Run with that thought of excitement. Keep telling yourself you are excited and see how that changes the way you approach the task or challenge.

58

"When one door of happiness closes, another opens, but often we look so long at the closed door that we do not see the one that has been opened for us."

- HELEN KELLER

The fact is, life is continuously changing. We have to get used to that. Dwelling on the past and the way things were and what has happened doesn't achieve anything.

Describing the natural selection mechanism, the Darwinian Evolutionary Theory was spot on (the theory states that individuals best adapted to their environments are more likely to survive and reproduce).[10] Charles Darwin theorised that the ones most responsive to change are the ones who survive. His theory relates to all areas of life - your relationship, your work, and even friendships. You must recognise that change is the only constant, and as such, you must let go of the past. Accept change, create change, and keep looking forward because that is the only way.

59

"If you give up now, you are declaring it will never happen."

— KEVIN M CAVANAGH

Put a bookmark on this page. On those days when your dream seems unreachable, read this again and again. We are all human. We ALL have moments of thinking we can't do this and that. Often, it is in those moments when you feel like giving up that you are closest to making a change.

Keep reminding yourself of the WHY you are doing what you are doing (you should have the why written alongside your goals). Find some small action that will move you even a tiny step towards your goal and do it today. Small actions will take you away from that place of 'I can't' and 'I want to give up.' Don't give up. You will feel so much better if you keep moving forward.

60

"Believe you can and you're halfway there."

— THEODORE ROOSEVELT

You've reached the 60th quote, so you are 66% of the way through this book, woohoo you! You are awesome for achieving that! I hope you are getting some value out of the book. Have you achieved any of your short-term goals? It would be great to know your feedback.

If you have missed a page, that's fine. We are all human, after all. Do try to go back and catch up, as the bit you missed might just be the gem that works for you! The other great thing to do at this point is to allocate time to review where you are going again. Are your goals still all relevant? Is your action plan working? Are you doing the actions you set (that is a sure-fire sign whether it is working or not)? Give yourself a big pat on the back. You are awesome. Keep reading, there are more gems ahead for you.

If you are faltering, a great way to get back on track is to go back to the beginning and look again at what you wrote down in your vision, purpose, and goals. Reconnect yourself with why you are doing this in the first place. That will help you get motivated and energised again.

Now, back to the quote. When elected just before his 43rd birthday, Theodore Roosevelt was the youngest American president in history. He reputedly had an incredible self-belief and confidence that he could be president. Believing in yourself is vital in enabling you to live your life to the fullest. Sometimes, it can be hard to see how things will get better. However, overcoming your mind and continually telling yourself that you can do it is the key. Keeping a note of small achievements is a great way to start building your confidence. It creates great momentum over time.

61

"You have one life don't waste it travelling somewhere you don't want to go."

- ANONYMOUS

As mentioned previously, on average, we lives 3754 weeks on this planet.[2] Can you afford to waste any of those? Many of us end up meandering through life, letting life lead us. We must decide what we want in life and, most importantly, make a plan to get us there.

Think of it this way; I happen to love road cycling. When I go out on a bike ride, I can either randomly ride around the neighbourhood with no plan of where I am going, or make a plan in advance of where I want to end up. I may find that some roads are closed and there are diversions I have to navigate, but I know exactly where my end destination is because I have planned it and I keep working towards it.

Life is the same, and this is why I encourage you to get super clear on what you want out of life. Visualize your goals each day and set off on your bike ride. When you have a direction and the plan to get you there, things become a lot clearer, and you stop wasting time with things that don't help you reach your destination.

62

"3 simple rules for life: If you do not go after what you want, you'll never have it. If you do not ask, the answer will always be no. If you do not step forward, you will always be in the same place."

- ANONYMOUS

The trick to success is not standing still. Yes, it is essential to pause, recognise when you have achieved a goal, take time to pat yourself on the back, and reflect on your success. However, don't stand still for too long. Remember, you won't achieve anything by sitting on the sofa, watching Netflix. Keep yourself busy working towards the next goal or challenge in your life.

Many of us are uncomfortable asking people for help or questioning things. The truth is that people are often flattered when you ask for their support. You get a different perspective that widens your thought process.

When I was young, I wasn't great at asking for help. Over the years, I have learnt that asking people for help is one of the best ways to achieve results quickly. Is there anyone in your network who can help you with a task? With who can you talk through a problem? A problem shared is a problem halved, as the old proverb goes.

63

"So far you have survived 100% of your worst days. You are doing great."

- NORM KELLY

My father used to have a saying that, 'Life is one damn thing after another.' I guess if you think about it, that is true. We are always faced with challenges to overcome. It is like nature's way of seeing who has the determination to continue and not give up.

Make yourself the person who never gives up. Intentionally choose never to give up. Write down some of the challenges you have already overcome in your life. Next time you come up against a big challenge, read what you have written down. It will act as a reminder and help build the belief that you can overcome challenges. That will shift your mindset to take on anything.

What challenges have I already overcome in life?

Think back and write down some challenges that you have faced and overcome in your life.

64

"Great things are achieved by a series of small things brought together."

- VINCENT VAN GOGH

Remarkable achievements are not attained through one big action. Vincent Van Gogh didn't paint sunflowers in one long day of working on it. In the same way, you won't get to your big scary goal in one leap, but in a series of smaller achievements.

It is excellent that you have written down some big scary goals. Nonetheless, the best way to achieve them is to break them down into smaller tasks. Physically tick off the small wins and remind yourself that each one is a step closer to that big scary goal. It helps you build momentum and belief. You will also feel great when you achieve something.

What small wins have I achieved that help me towards my goals?

Write them down here to remind yourself that you are making progress.

65

"I love sleep. My life has the tendency to fall apart when I'm awake, you know?"

- ERNEST HEMINGWAY

Before Edison invented the lightbulb in 1879, the average person went to bed at sunset and slept eleven hours a night.[11] Research suggests that if we get less than 7 hours of sleep, our prefrontal cortex gets less blood flow, leading to reduced ability to make the right decisions. What does that mean? Sleep matters!

Make yourself a daily bedtime routine. Ideally, you should go to bed at roughly the same time each night. Plan your routine like you would for a child. We take great effort to get our kids to bed at the same time each night—they get downtime with a bath, reading to settle them, dim lighting, etc. As adults, we would benefit from this type of routine too. However, we often neglect to do this.

I won't go into great details about circadian rhythms as that is not the purpose of this book. Just take on board that you can't be successful if you don't look after your body and mind, and sleep is a big part of that.

My daily bedtime routine plan.

Create a relaxing bedtime routine that works for you. Write it down here to make it something to which you commit.

> "The greatest weapon against stress is our ability to choose one thought over another."

— WILLIAM JAMES

Many of us experience stress at some point in our work or personal lives. How we deal with it is a personal choice. We either let it consume us, or we learn to control it. If two cars are in a traffic jam, one driver may get completely stressed out by the situation, the other not at all.

There are short-term things you can do to relieve stress immediately:

Reduce your consumption of sugar and drinks containing caffeine and alcohol.

- Do physical exercise to metabolize stress hormones and restore your body and mind to a calmer, more relaxed state.
- Get more sleep. Don't go to bed too late and create a relaxing routine before bedtime. It will help calm your brain.
- Talking to a friend or colleague can release some of your stress. The act of talking out loud not only shares problems but also helps your mind process them.
  Find time to relax and switch off. Self-care is important. Find time to read, have a bath, try gardening, baking, do yoga!
- Practice gratitude. What are you grateful for in your day?

If you regularly suffer from stress, this could have a severe impact on your health in the long run. Believe me, I have seen this happen. You need to address the causes. Is it a belief? Are you in a situation that you are unhappy with or you can't control?

Is your diet contributing to your stress? Start journaling to capture what gets under your skin so you can quickly identify these problems. Take control. Write down the problem and come up with as many possible solutions as you can. Choose a solution and write what will be done, by when, and how. It gives you a clear, actionable plan to address stressful problems.

What things make me stressed?

List the things here that wind you up and make you stressed.

67

"For you to win, you must be willing to get up every time you fail. Failure should not discourage you from achieving what you set out to do."

- MICHAEL JORDAN

When you feel like quitting, remember why you started in the first place. We are all human, and, naturally, there are moments when we feel like quitting. With this book, you are on a journey, and you have come far. What a waste it would be to give that up now, right?

There are moments in life when we all feel like quitting because that seems to be the easiest option. If we practice being positive, pushing ourselves on, encouraging ourselves to keep going, we would get through failures and achieve our dreams. When you feel like quitting, find one small thing you can do, one small task that will move you even slightly towards your goals. Focus on that task like it's the most important thing in the world. It will help get you back on track. Don't give up on yourself.

68

"Clear your mind. It doesn't matter how bright the path is, if your mind is always cloudy."

- ANONYMOUS

Imagine doing a spring clean on your mind. If you are like me and have thousands of thoughts spinning around your head, it can be challenging to make progress. You should regularly take time to declutter your mind.

There are many ways to achieve this. I found that exercise works exceptionally well, so does meditation and simply giving yourself some uninterrupted time to make decisions.

Physically clearing the excess clutter on your desk (or the environment where you tend to work) helps too. According to the Harvard Business Review, our physical environments significantly influence our cognition, emotions, and behaviour. As a result, it affects our decision-making too.[12]

Work out what things work for you. When you clear your mind, you will be more effective.

69

"Accept responsibility for your life. Know that it is you who will get you where you want to go, no one else."

- LES BROWN

Take full responsibility for yourself. Don't compare or blame others. The only person that can change your life is you. Sadly, no one is going to come along with a wand and magically give you the life of your dreams. You need to choose what you want in life and then commit to making it happen yourself.

Intentionally take responsibility for your life. If you take action whilst reading this book, things will change in your life. You need to find the drive and determination to keep going for days, then weeks, then months. Only you can choose which way to go. Once you have made up your mind, don't let others lead your life.

70

"Worry is like a rocking chair; It gives you something to do, But doesn't get you anywhere."

- ERMA BOMBECK

Sometimes, we just can't help it. Something troubles us or causes us to worry. In truth, worry doesn't help you. It saps all your energy and keeps your mind from finding a solution.

Worry tricks your mind. You may think you are dealing with something when, in fact, you are not. You are just worrying about it, going round and round but not moving forward. Often worry comes from the feeling of not being in control.

There was an interesting study at Cornell University. In the study, scientists found that, firstly, 85% of what we worry about never happens. Secondly, of the 15% of the worries that did happen, 79% of the subjects discovered that they could handle the difficulty better than expected. The conclusion is that 97% of our worries are baseless and result from an unfounded pessimistic perception.[13]

So what should we do to address worries? The first thing to do is acknowledging that something is worrying you. Then it would help if you worked actively on solving the problem. One technique is to take three deep breaths, reset your mind and then look at it again. See if you can see a clearer, more objective view about your worries. Talking to someone often helps too. So, you might as well share your worries with a trusted companion.

71

"Even if you are on the right track, you'll get run over if you just sit there."

- WILL ROGERS

I have worked in the technology industry for years. When developing computer software, engineers don't just build it all in one go and bang it is all done. They produce what is known as a minimum viable product, the minimum needed to get it working and useful. Then, they continually iterate and look for ways to improve it.

Apply the same approach to yourself. Look to continually improve yourself and iterate over and over again. You might feel that you are doing well and things are heading in the right direction. Don't settle for that. Imagine how better things would be if you can keep improving forever! Continually working on achieving small improvements will build up momentum to a massive change in the long run. Commit to continuously working on yourself; do not let yourself stand still.

72

"Don't let your past screw up your future."

- KEVIN M CAVANAGH

I'm referencing the past again as we all have one. Some of it will be good and some we consider bad. If you can't let go of your past and look forward to a better one, you will never achieve the change and the better life that you so desire. We need to be accepting. Not accepting that it was good or bad, but accept that the past has already happened and cannot be changed.

The most useful thing we can do is learn from past experiences as a baseline for improvements. Look at your goals again, look forward to the future you want and visualize what that will look like. The best way to forget the past is to keep your mind busy and concentrate on your future.

73

"Love yourself first and everything else falls into line. You really have to love yourself to get anything done in this world."

- LUCILLE BALL

Many of us are too hard on ourselves and continually criticize ourselves internally. Loving yourself starts with actually liking yourself. Liking yourself begins with respecting yourself, and that begins with being kind to yourself. If you can shift your mindset to love yourself, it will profoundly impact you for the rest of your life.

Praise yourself for the good things you do each day, no matter how small they are. At the end of each day, write down one good thing about yourself. Build this over time, and you will start to see the positive impact of loving yourself.

74

"If you do not go after what you want, you will never have it."

- NORA ROBERTS

Have you ever wondered why some people fall apart when times are hard, while others manage to keep moving forward?

When there is a natural disaster like a hurricane or earthquake, the victims all suffer the same loss. Yet some people cannot cope with the situation. In contrast, others will go through grieving, then pick themselves up and begin moving on, rebuilding both emotionally and physically.

I have never experienced that level of despair, so I can only speak from my personal experience of coming through several tragedies and still having the desire to keep moving forward. I'm no stronger than any of you, I've just learnt to carry the load differently.

Remember, it is always your choice. When you experience hard times or when anything happens – you can choose how you will respond. Will you choose to be the victim and hold on to thoughts like "why do bad things always happen to me?" or "there's no way I can get through this!"? Or will you choose to think "this is a real challenge, a difficult situation, but I will not let it defeat me." My eldest son taught me a phrase he likes to use; "I don't know how to do this YET." Use this approach that you may not know what to do yet, but you have everything inside you to find a solution.

It is not all about you either. There are often others that depend on us, and this can be powerful motivation! We live in families and communities. How we respond to situations impacts the lives of others. You don't have to shoulder the load all by yourself. Enlist others' help and look at how you can help others with their loads too.

It is all about how you view your world. If the load your carrying hasn't killed you, there must be a reason for you to carry it. Maybe it's teaching you or preparing you for something. Know you will eventually get through it if you don't give up. The current situation will not last forever. Life can be hard, really hard. However, it's not the load that breaks you. It's the way you carry it.

75

"Only do what your heart tells you."

— DIANA, PRINCESS OF WALES

Deep down in all of us, we all know when we are doing something that is not right for us. It can be something you have been doing for a day, a week, or maybe years. Take a moment today to sit with no distractions and ask yourself what things you are doing that are not right for you. You will know in your heart what they are.

Once you have identified one or maybe several things, write them down and start working on changing them. It doesn't necessarily mean giving up on them. For instance, if you are not enjoying your job, it doesn't always mean quitting the company. Could there be other roles in the same company that may be more suitable for you? When we open our eyes to possibility, we often see that the answers are in front of us. Be guided by your heart.

Things currently in my life that are not right for me right now.

Write down one or two things that you know deep down are not right.

76

"The best time to plant a tree was 20 years ago, the second best time is now."

- CHINESE PROVERB

Wouldn't it be great to have a time machine and go back 20 years, with all the knowledge you have now? To start creating your dream life 20 years ago, imagine where you would be now? Sadly, this is not an option!

However, you mustn't let another 20 years drift by. Don't let one more year or even another month pass by before you take action. You can't change the past, but you can impact your future right now.

77

"People are never sorry they failed, they are sorry they didn't try."

- ANONYMOUS

If you sat there cursing your long commute, berating the boss you don't get along with, or moaning about what money you don't have, here is something for you; no one cares. It may sound harsh but it's true, no one cares about any of the challenges you have. You need to pick yourself up and try to make the change for yourself.

Zoom forward for a moment and visualize yourself on your death bed. What conversation would you prefer to have with your children or grandchildren? I never tried because I was too afraid, or I failed many times but had a fulfilled life trying. Push yourself to try and see what amazing things can happen.

78

"All progress takes place outside the comfort zone."

- MICHAEL JOHN BOBAK

As mentioned, some people are happy to live their entire lives inside their comfort zone. As you have read this book so far, you are clearly not one of them. To progress at anything, we have to push ourselves outside our comfort zone.

Remember back when you were a child? How many times did you push yourself outside your comfort zone? What was the worst thing that ever happened? A grazed knee when you fell off your bike whilst learning? We all have these imaginary boundaries, but they are just that, imaginary. Bust through yours and see where it could lead you.

79

"If you work just for money, you'll never make it, but if you love what you're doing and you always put the customer first, success will be yours."

- RAY KROC

In today's world, it is far too easy to get sucked into chasing the money. It becomes a trap, and the more you earn, the greater your reliance on that level of earning. You get one go at this life. If you don't love what you are doing, either find a new way of doing it, change your perspective, or change it completely.

Putting aside the customer element of this quote, following your dream or your real passion will always make you more successful in life. Love what you are doing, don't just do a job for the money because doing so will ultimately leave you feeling unfulfilled. If you can achieve this, it will be easy to put the customer first, whoever that customer may be.

80

"Motivation gets you going, but discipline keeps you growing."

- JOHN C. MAXWELL

Often when we start something new, we begin with a tremendous amount of enthusiasm and inspiration. A few days or weeks later, that enthusiasm reduces, and you need something else to keep you going. Enthusiasm may get us started, but discipline is what sees us through. Self-discipline is the secret ingredient of success. It is the link between goals and accomplishments. Self-discipline has been referenced time and time again by those who have accomplished great things.

So, how do you build self-discipline? You need to develop it into a habit. For example, if your goal is to write more, don't just choose to write on the days when you feel great. Instead, make a habit of writing every day regardless of how you feel. Don't let your emotions take charge. Use the logical part of your brain to be disciplined, and write each day.

Put simply, if you don't have self-discipline, you will not succeed. Conversely, if you learn to be disciplined with your daily actions, you will achieve anything you set your mind to.

81

"Low self-esteem is like driving through life with your hand-break on."

- MAXWELL MALTZ

As you improve yourself, there will be some days when you don't automatically jump out of bed feeling amazing. No one feels fantastic every single day; that is not real life. The trick is to notice the days when your self-esteem feels low, when you can't get up, nothing feels right, and you can't get going. Just as a car can't drive at full speed with the handbrake on, your progress is hampered by constant negative thoughts and beliefs if you have low self-esteem.

Nobody is born with limitless self-confidence. If someone seems to have incredible self-esteem, it's usually because they have worked on building it for years.

Write down ten good things about you today and hide them away until you have a bad day. Then, when you need it, look at it and remind yourself how awesome you are. It also works to look at your goals, reminding yourself of where you are heading and why. Your brain needs this fuel to keep it positive and on track.

Getting to know yourself and appreciating your unique and exceptional qualities helps you develop strong self-esteem.

10 good things about me to build my self-esteem.

Write ten good things about you. If you struggle, ask someone for some good things they see in you.

82

"Ability is what you're capable of doing. Motivation determines what you do. Attitude determines how well you do it."

- LOU HOLTZ

Ability, motivation, and attitude are three key ingredients to help you achieve your life goals. These three are all needed to achieve success.

Ability is about your skills. What can you do? What's your unique talent? What is it that you are so good at that people ask you to do it all the time?

Motivation is your why. Why you do what you do? What makes you get up in the morning? Why do you keep going? What's the vision you're working towards? What's your inspiration?

Attitude is how you feel when doing something. It determines how high and how far you will go. Creating and keeping a positive attitude will help you in all areas of your life.

People with a positive attitude often appear to have more energy, are self-confident, and hopeful. They tend to set higher goals and expend more effort to reach their goals. Attitude is an important attribute you should work on. Your attitude drives you to better your abilities, focus on the positive, look for opportunities, and take action on everything!

83

"Life is really simple, but we insist on making it complicated."

- CONFUCIUS

This is never truer than in the digital world, with the 24/7 Internet lifestyles we lead. When you strip it back to basics, life is straightforward. We have simple needs: water, food, shelter and companionship. One challenge that makes our lives over-complicated in the digital age is information overload. Rarely is our problem a lack of accessible information, it's complicated by too much information. All the information in our heads can impact our effectiveness. We begin to feel like a hamster in a wheel, going round and round and getting nowhere.

Let me give you the analogy of the humble sandwich shop. Thirty years ago, a sandwich shop typically sold a basic selection of sandwiches and drinks. Today, many sandwich shops sell sandwiches with every filling you can imagine, wraps, soups, jacket potatoes, salads, cakes, snacks, smoothies, fruit, the list is endless. Have you ever been in a queue in a sandwich shop, with someone at the front agonizing over what options to order?

Whilst having all these options and choices can be beneficial, if they exist in every area of our lives, it causes an information overload that stops our mind thinking clearly. With too much information floating around your head, it's almost impossible to know what to focus on.

As mentioned previously, meditation is a great way to clear your mind and get back to keeping things simple. Build meditation into your daily plan and practice it daily. Even if it is for just 5 minutes, invest that time in yourself. Clear your mind and work on keeping your thoughts simple.

.

84

"Limits exist only in your mind."

- ANONYMOUS

We all develop beliefs in our minds about what we can and can't achieve. Whether that is physical limits, financial limits, or emotional limits. These limits are often formed at an early age, transmitted from parents, friends and people in authority. These limits become coded in our brain and become our default. We listen to what we tell ourselves and allow ourselves to believe it's true. We subconsciously live up to these limits.

It all starts with thoughts. What we think determines how we act and what we will become. When you stop putting negative limitations on yourself, everything becomes possible. The only limit you have is the one you are creating. The reality is we can all do things we don't think we can do.

Next time you become aware of a negative limit, reset your mind and actively find a positive alternative. Try repeating that positive alternative to yourself several times (I will do this; I am capable etc.). Write it down and put it somewhere you will see every day and keep practicing it. It will take time, but you will smash through these limits and expand your mind and life.

85

"Always be a first rate version of yourself and not a second rate version of someone else."

- JUDY GARLAND

If you have come this far, you are doing an awesome job. Pat yourself on the back and give yourself a high five in the mirror. A bit of self-praise is always good for you. Imagine what else you can achieve if you strive to be the best you can be? Doesn't it feel great to be on the road to being the best version of you?

In a world of almost 8 billion people, it never ceases to amaze me that we are all born unique. There is no mass production of identical people; we are all born individuals. Don't look to copy what somebody else is doing, but be the real amazing you. Be proud of yourself and what you are achieving.

As we reach the end of this book, you need to work out what next? You could start over and work through the book again. Ensure you continue to work on your unique plan to make you the best you can be. Using your healthy mindset, you will be able to tackle anything in life.

86

"From my weakness, I drew strength that never left me."

- JORGE LUIS BORGES

We all have weaknesses in us. Do you think successful people would have made it had they not overcome their weaknesses? As my eldest son (at the age of 10) once expressed to me, 'Your weakness is your strength.' They are part of your belief system. It can be hard to accept that what you believe to be a fact is often an opinion or learned belief. If you break down that perceived fact, you can learn that there is a possible new way of thinking to get better results.

Tai Lopez used the example of a monkey. Once a monkey is put into a zoo, it gets depressed because it feels helpless to hunt for its own food and control its own destiny. Even when you take that monkey out of the cage and return it to the jungle, it usually will still act helpless and just sit and starve to death. It doesn't realize that it's no longer helpless now that it's out of the zoo cage.[14]

The good news is that you don't have to be that monkey. You may have a weakness now, but it doesn't have to continue to be a weakness. It is never too late to change something. Treat your weaknesses like a to-do list, identify them and take steps to make them your strengths. Look at them as a means to grow and change. This principle applies to work and our personal life. Work on your weaknesses to make them your strengths.

87

"Start creating the reality of your tomorrow today."

- KEVIN M CAVANAGH

Focus on starting, not finishing. We've focused a lot on your goals. Setting goals is a significant step, and visualizing them helps make them feel real. What new goals will you set when you finish this book? What new challenges lie ahead for you? Here is a cold hard fact; if you take no further action, nothing will change.

Start creating your tomorrow today. Stop saying you don't have time. If you prioritize yourself and your future, you will make the time and make it happen.

The first step is always the hardest. It is about starting and building momentum. Imagine a snowball rolling down a hill. It starts small, gets bigger and bigger, and as the momentum grows, it gets stronger and faster. Could this be you, heading towards your big goal? Reward yourself for each step forward. When you commit to yourself and start, amazing things happen.

88

"You are what you eat."

- VICTOR LINDLAHR

At first glance, it may seem a little odd to have a quote about food in this book, but hear me out. This quote originates from the French lawyer Anthelme Brillat-Savarin, who in 1826 wrote, "Dis-moi ce que tu manges, je te dirai ce que tu es." (Tell me what you eat and I will tell you what you are.) The quote was adapted and used by Victor Lindlahr in his radio talks in the 1930s. His view was that ninety percent of the diseases known to man, as well as low mood and low motivation, are caused by cheap foodstuffs.[15]

Naturally, what you eat affects your body physically. Interestingly, it affects your mood too. Studies have found that our diet can have a significant impact on our mood and general well-being. It is a vast area, and I don't intend to get into too much detail. That being said, limiting sugar and eating more fruits and vegetables are the simple things you can do to give yourself more energy, boost your mood, and improve your focus.

Back in the first COVID-19 lockdown, my wife attended several online nutrition workshops. As a result, our family decided to change our diet; cutting down on sugar, wheat, processed foods and meat. Not to mention packing in lots more fruit and vegetables. I can genuinely say it has improved our energy levels, helped us deal with stress better, feel more positive and I would even argue it makes your skin look better - I'm sure I look ten years younger!

Take time this week to look at what you eat. What are the small steps you can take to improve what you eat? Remember that it has a significant impact on your body and mind.

89

"Success is the sum of small efforts — repeated day in and day out."

- ROBERT COLLIER

Success doesn't happen overnight. It takes a lot of perseverance and patience, and it's more of a journey. First, you have to build that strong solid foundation as nothing will be accomplished without this. Next, you need to put in effort daily, no matter how small, to achieve success.

If you want more from life, but you come home from work, sit on the couch, and just watch TV, you do not show the self-control to achieve more. Every day think to yourself, 'What can I and must I do today to get myself closer to success?'

Remember, success doesn't just equate to money earned. Success is becoming a better you. It is about happiness and enjoying the life you have whilst you are here on this planet. Measure your success and your achievement of goals not just on financial gain, but also on the improvements you are making in yourself, your life, and your mindset.

90

"You haven't come this far to only come this far."

- ANONYMOUS

If you followed the tools and strategies in this book, you unquestionably have come a long way. But that doesn't mean you can stop here. Keep practicing these skills and techniques. Remember, on average, we get 3754 weeks on this planet, so don't let the time you have invested reading this book be wasted. If you've been reading but not taking action, now is the time to start!

- Keep setting yourself goals and challenge yourself.
- Continue working on any mind limiting beliefs you may have.
- Unleash your positivity on the world.
- Imagine what you could turn the rest of your life into.
- Push yourself further and further.
- Awaken your dreams and work towards them.

Create the life you always wanted and become the amazing person you were destined to become.

A final word

My passion is to live a happy and fulfilling life. My purpose is to inspire people to be the best they can be in their lives. The whole reason for writing this book was to encourage people to change their mindset and push them to take action to improve their lives.

I want to thank you for sticking with this book through the 90 quotes. If I've had any impact on your life, then it's been worthwhile writing this book!

Understand that life is a journey crafted by you. Make sure you take the time to enjoy your journey instead of just rush along, focusing on the end destination. There will be ups and downs. Be prepared for the downs, stay positive, and enjoy the ups while they last.

Take the time to share nuggets of this book with friends, relatives, and colleagues that you think would benefit from it. It is never too late for anyone, so let's get life-changing positivity out there. Imagine if we could all improve our lives, beliefs, and mindset, then this world would be even more incredible than it already is.

We can forget over time, so keep reminding yourself of the tools and strategies in this book. Make it the platform from which you leap and grow into the amazing person you already are.

References

1. Zuckerman Catherine, National Geographic - Science 101 report,
2. World Health Organisation - Life expectancy and Healthy life expectancy survey
3. Racy Famira, The Inner Speech Lab at Mount Royal University, Canada
4. Chopra Deepak, Quantum Healing Exploring the Frontiers of Mind/body Medicine, Revised and updated Edition 2015
5. Brown Eileen, ZDNET.com - Americans spend far more time on their smartphones than they think, April 2019
6. For additional resources see www.kevinmcavanagh.com/resources
7. Gallup World Poll - The World's Broken Workplace, 2017
8. Pease Allan & Barbara, The Definitive Book of Body Language, 2017
9. Hurley James, The Times - Olderpreneurs' insist retiring is for wimps, 2017
10. Darwin Charles, On the Origin of Species, 1859
11. Curry Arwen, How Electric Light Changed the Night, 2015
12. Sander Libby, Harvard Business Review - The Case for Finally Cleaning Your Desk
13. Leahy Robert L, Study of Cornell University, 2005

14. Lopez Tai, Entrepreneur magazine - How to Live the Good Life, April 2017
15. Hamblin James, The Atlantic - Strength and Vigor Depend on What You Eat, 2014

About the Author

Kevin M Cavanagh works in the technology industry, having read business studies at university. Throughout his life, Kevin has always been interested in the idea and practice of positivity, and the mind's inherent power to inspire and motivate.

A depth of life experience has shaped his positive motivational approach. His learned ability to rise to challenges and take on new goals has been evident many times whilst living in Britain, Canada and Denmark, cheating death in Hawaii, and becoming marooned on a prison island whilst sailing in a storm in the Indian Ocean on his honeymoon.

In 2020, at the height of the COVID-19 pandemic, Kevin began writing his debut book. The crisis prompted many people to re-evaluate their lives and look for motivation and mindset techniques to stay positive despite the challenges. Wanting to share the tools and techniques he had learned throughout his life, Kevin started writing this book to share positivity and motivation with others.

Born and raised in Lancashire, Kevin now lives with his wife and two boys in Buckinghamshire.

Kevin also has a keen interest in disruptive technology and has worked alongside tech giants like Microsoft and Amazon to help government departments transform services through digital technology.

Outside of his role in the technology industry, Kevin coaches a junior football team and enjoys swimming, cycling, reading, and as a hobby, working with people as a mindset coach.

You can reach Kevin on:

LinkedIn: @kevinmcavanagh
Twitter: @kevinmcavanagh
Instagram: @kevinmcavanagh
Email: kevin@kevinmcavanagh.com
Website: www.kevinmcavanagh.com

One last thing...

thank you

I'd love to hear how you got on with the book? You can get in touch on social media or through my website www.kevinmcavanagh.com.

Please leave a book review!
If you enjoyed the book, I would be grateful if you would leave an honest review on Amazon or wherever you purchased it.

Every review matters, and it matters to me a *lot!*

Thank you
Kevin M Cavanagh

Printed in Great Britain
by Amazon